100 PROOF PURE

OLD JESS

JESSE HELMS QUOTED

Compiled and Published by *the insider*
A division of The News and Observer Publishing Co.

100 Proof Pure, Old Jess

Cover illustration and editorial cartoons

by Dwane Powell,

editorial cartoonist for   in Raleigh, N.C.

Some quotations come from:

VIEWPOINT editorial broadcast on WRAL-TV from 1960 - 1972.

<u>When</u> <u>Free</u> <u>Men</u> <u>Shall</u> <u>Stand:</u> <u>A</u> <u>Sobering</u> <u>Look</u> <u>at</u> <u>the</u> <u>Supertaxing,</u>
<u>Superspending</u> <u>Superbureaucracy</u> <u>in</u> <u>Washington,</u>
by U.S. Senator Jesse Helms, 1976.

ISBN 0-935400-18-4

Printed in Raleigh, North Carolina
Second Printing, January 1995

100 PROOF PURE
OLD JESS

Jesse Helms' thoughts on…

MORALS

"Well there are a lot of number one problems in America. But let me boil it down to two. One is the federal debt, the interest, the wild spending by the left-wing members of Congress for 40 years. ..., The other number one problem ... is the dire need that we restore the moral and religious principles to this country of ours, and restore the family as the keystone of our society."

— News & Observer, 10/21/90

"I think all of us wish he hadn't done it ... he assured us he hasn't touched it [marijuana] since then. ... I suspect that everyone on the high court has broken one law or another."

— on Supreme Court nominee Douglas Ginsburg; Washington Post, 11/6/87

"The subject matter is so obscene, so revolting, it's difficult for me to stand here and talk about it. I may throw up."

— on an AIDS prevention comic book; Los Angeles Times, 10/14/87

"If America is to survive, there must be an American reawakening. We cannot continue down this destructive path or we will duplicate the fall of Rome and all other beaten civilizations in history. Before it is too late, we must have the courage and the decency to stand up for life, the family and all other principles that made this nation great."

— News & Observer, 1/22/93

"The problem is that millions of families refuse to subscribe to those movie channels because they do not want their children to be exposed to the violence, the disgusting dialogue and the sexually explicit scenes so prevalent."
— *News & Observer, 2/1/92*

"I am here tonight to suggest that the American taxpayers have no interest, and the federal government has no business, supporting or assisting in the slightest degree any organization that uses its tax-deductible donations in efforts to blackmail the Boy Scouts of America into accepting homosexuals and/or atheists within their ranks, or to force the Boy Scouts of America to drop their members' pledge to God and country."
— *News & Observer, 9/19/92*

4

"I think God is giving this country one more chance to save itself. What's going on in this country, what is being condoned...if something doesn't happen in this country, maybe we ought to apologize to Sodom and Gomorrah."
— News & Observer, 10/14/90

"It just disturbs the sensibility of decent people. This is not just a different lifestyle we're talking about here. This is sodomy."
— News & Observer, 1/30/93

"Common sense dictates that (marriage) licenses be denied to those suffering from AIDS."
— Los Angeles Times, 5/22/87

"What is really at stake is whether the American people will allow the cultural high ground of this nation to sink into the slime of an abyss just to placate people who seek to destroy the Judeo-Christian values of this country."

— *News & Observer, 10/25/90*

"Southerners are good basic people. They believe in the Bible. They follow the teachings of God. Most of them strive to be like Jesus. And as long as the Republican Party attempts to work within the scope of his teachings, it will win."

— *speech, Winston-Salem, 10/78*

"These funds are being allocated to fund research and treatment of AIDS not because of its threat to society, but on the basis of media hype and who can make the loudest noise in the halls of Congress."

— News & Observer, 10/23/90

"There are entirely too many clergymen who can hardly differentiate between the Seventh Commandment and the Fifth Amendment. For many parents, the Bill of Rights is a debt to be paid next year sometime, and the Bible is a dust-catcher in the living room bookrack."

— Viewpoint, 8/27/65

"Americans need to stop protesting, marching, looting, burning, destroying, threatening, posturing and loafing. They need to start minding their own business again, go back to work, regain respect for decency and personal responsibility, and to pray for God's forgiveness for what they have deliberately tried to do to America."

— *Viewpoint, 8/4/66*

" A handful of determined atheists and agnostics, in collection with a handful of Pharisees on the Supreme Court, succeeded in their great aim of using the power of law to eradicate all mention of God and His Word in every public school classroom in America."

— *When Free Men Shall Stand, p. 108, 1976*

"The public schools have been going downhill morally and academically since the Supreme Court outlawed school prayer."

— Charlotte Observer, 1/26/92

"As the Supreme Court has rephrased the words of Tiny Tim, 'May a legally accepted secular equivalent bless us, every one.'"

— Viewpoint, 12/17/62

FOREIGN POLICY

"The Senate needs to wake up and smell the coffee— America is in gravest mortal danger and we should abrogate the ABM Treaty (because it is) impeding our ability to defend our supreme national interests."

— *Washington Post, 4/13/87*

"The State Department and the CIA are constantly trying to discredit me, and they're not going to be able to do it. ... If they want to play the game of intimidation, of harassment and of leaks, we'll meet them right in the middle of the field."

— *Los Angeles Times, 8/4/86*

"Unfortunately the Egyptian-Israeli peace treaty negotiated by President Carter in exhausting circumstances appears not to be, in fact, a peace treaty at all, but merely an expedient decision by both Israel and Egypt to extend the military truce which has prevailed in the Middle East since 1973. In character, it is much closer to the disengagement agreement."

— *News & Observer*, 4/22/79

"It's poppycock. They're (State Department officials) trying to silence me. They don't like the fact I'm opposed to their little agenda down there (in Chile), which is to sell out the U.S."

— *Los Angeles Times*, 8/5/86

"We need only examine the documents of time to see that even the estimable Pilgrim fathers had some alien ideas tucked away in their own baggage. You might even go so far as to say that communism came over on the Mayflower."

— *When Free Men Shall Stand, p.22, 1976*

"The Union of Soviet Socialist Republics as we came to know it is collapsing from within, from internal decay caused by despotic tyranny. But a troubling sense of euphoria has settled on some of our citizens—some politicians, editors, so-called pundits. Let me tell you something. It's not all over. Communism is not dead. The threat has not disappeared."

— *News & Observer, 9/29/91*

"The internal torment in America has been carefully contrived by enemies of America to break the spirit and will of the country, so as to weaken us in our resistance to the spread of communism around the world."

— Viewpoint, 2/20/68

"The problem is, we are ignoring our friends around the world and trying to co-exist with an atheistic, communistic movement, trying to buy time when we ought to be standing up with and for people who believe in freedom."

— Charlotte Observer, 10/19/78

"If the situation in Mexico continues to be one of fraud, corruption and the strangling of democracy, then vast infusions of U.S. taxpayers' cash will only open up more opportunities for corruption and fraud."

— Washington Post, 6/18/86

"To be sure, Africa is largely uncivilized. There is support for the contention that the United Nations has moved too rapidly in creating nations...which are not ready for independence."

—Viewpoint 1961, (Raleigh Times, 11/1/84)

"The idea that we can take anything the Soviets have to offer in good faith is dangerous nonsense."

— Los Angeles Times, 9/18/87

15

"We adopted 26 amendments in one hour—quite some sausage-making, a measure of broad discontent among senators with the State Department. We're not supposed to be a bunch of eunuchs in foreign policy, and I won't be."

— *Washington Post, 10/11/87*

"As long as I am chairman, there will be no vindictiveness permitted. No getting even. ... My first priority this morning should be to assure you of my intent to work with you in the spirit of mutual friendship and cooperation."

— *News & Observer, 11/10/94, in a letter to Sec. of State Warren Christopher*

"If you agree (to delay a vote on GATT), Mr. President, I can assure that it will have an exceedingly positive effect on my making certain that the administration positions on all foreign policy matters during the 104th Congress will be considered fully and fairly,"

— Associated Press, 11/16, from a letter to President Clinton

"This whole peace process over there is a fraud and you'd better look carefully at what's going on," he said. ``Syria doesn't want peace. They want the Golan Heights. They want access to the pocketbooks of the American taxpayers."

— New York Times, 11/19/94

17

"The foreign aid program has spent an estimated $2 trillion of the American taxpayers' money, much of it going down foreign rat-holes, to countries that constantly oppose us in the United Nations, and many which rejected concepts of freedom."

— *New York Times, 11/13/94*

``All citizens should heed the axiom that politics should unfailingly stop at the water's edge. ...For my part, I thank the Lord that as of this moment, no American has lost his life in the strange drama unfolding in the miserable piece of geography known as Haiti."

— *Associated Press, 9/2/94*

18

THE FAMOUS

THE ULTRA-LEFT, FAT, COMMIE PINKO SENATOR FROM MASSACHUSETTS AND THE ULTRA-RIGHT, WALL-EYED, REGRESSIVE SENATOR FROM NORTH CAROLINA SUDDENLY REALIZED THAT THEY WERE SHARING A FOXHOLE.

"Because she's a damn lesbian."
> — on opposing HUD Asst. Sec. Roberta
> Achtenberg; News & Observer, 5/6/93

"She's not your garden-variety lesbian. She's a militant-activist-mean lesbian, working her whole career to advance the homosexual agenda."
> — on HUD Assistant Secretary Roberta Achtenberg;
> News & Observer, 5/8/93

"The State Department did not want to disturb Mr. Shevardnadze with the sounds of democracy, to which Mr. Shevardnadze is not accustomed at home in the Soviet Union."
> — New York Times, 10/01/87

"I am sort of a middleman between the American farmer and Dick Lugar and Ted Kennedy—an odd couple if I ever saw one."

— Los Angeles Times, 10/2/87

"The civil-rights movement, as Dr. King calls it, has had an uncommon number of moral degenerates leading the parade. Bayard Rustin, who directed the 'March on Washington' in 1963, is a self-confessed homosexual who served time in jail for a sordid offense. James Baldwin, the Negro author and widely advertised authority on civil rights, cannot get his mind out of the sewer, if one may judge from the literary efforts."

— Viewpoint, 4/1/65

"There have been 248 different U.S. senators in the 18 years and five months I have been there. None—none—have been more capable than Dan Quayle."

— News & Observer, 6/4/91

"It is interesting to note that the Nobel Peace Prize won't be awarded this year. When one recalls that Martin Luther King got the prize last year, it may be just as well that the committee decided not to award one this year. Perhaps it was too difficult to choose between Stokely Carmichael and Ho Chi Minh."

— Viewpoint, 10/26/66

"It was President Reagan who rightly termed the Soviet Union 'the evil empire.' Despite [Soviet leader Mikhail S.] Gorbachev's reputation as a man of peace, his administration has been characterized by phenomenal preparations for war."

— *News & Observer, 10/11/90*

"I've never exploited the issue before...that is why the ultra liberal editors say: 'Racism racism.' They say it was racism because some of us opposed the Martin Luther King holiday. Well, I opposed it, yes. But, I was on the Senate floor this week praising (Doug Wilder) the governor of Virginia."

— *The Hotline, 5/10/90*

"All of this business of giving Saddam Hussein the encouragement and the time he needs, we're just a bunch of suckers to do that."

— *News & Observer, 12/1/90*

"Some people in politics can dish it, but they can't take it. The gentleman (Democratic opponent Harvey Gantt) was caught with his rants and his raves down."

— *News & Observer, 9/8/90*

"I'll go to my grave regretting that Robert Bork did not get the seat on the U.S. Supreme Court which he so richly deserved."

— *News & Observer, 10/8/93*

"Millions of Americans, and senators, watched television and witnessed with disgust the vilification by hearsay of Clarence Thomas. Senators piously professed to believe Anita Hill, and Senator Kennedy, of all people, sitting in judgment of this man. There has never been a scintilla of bona fide evidence against him."

— News & Observer, 11/11/94

"I think it was a tragedy that he got enmeshed in the Watergate affair. Nixon was one of the brightest presidents we had."

— News & Observer, 4/23/94

LIBERALS

"The U.S. National Survey has released some statistics showing the married men live longer and healthier lives than bachelors. Which shows, we suppose, that if a gal's cooking doesn't measure up, or if her allure isn't luring, and if she can't get a man with a gun— she ought to try using statistics."

— Viewpoint, 1/11/63

"The Clinton administration is headed down a slippery slope in health care reform because it is focusing on a phantom problem. The president claims that there are 37 million Americans without health insurance. This does not mean that 37 million Americans don't get health care."

— Letter to the editor; News & Observer, 8/28/93

"We live in the greatest country that the Lord has ever created. ...But we are in danger of letting go of the fundamental principles of this country. Anytime you have a Senate race which is paid for, orchestrated and controlled by homosexuals and lesbians and the labor unions and the People for the American Way, and the ACLU, and all the rest of them, you are in danger of losing your liberties."

— *News & Observer, 11/2/90*

"The Senate is a Republican Senate by a narrow margin. But it is not a conservative Senate. To prevent Ronald Reagan from having to take half a loaf, we need seven to 10 more conservatives."

— *Los Angeles Times, 2/18/86*

"The liberals want to raise taxes here and raise taxes there. The point is we don't need any new taxes. We need to reduce federal spending...Teddy Kennedy and all the other liberal senators know how to solve problems, they think. They throw your money at it."
— *News & Observer, 10/14/90*

"'Equality' is the process of denying another man his property right by Supreme Court edict. And 'responsibility' is merely a matter of doing anything you want to do—just as long as you persuade yourself that it's all right."
— *Viewpoint, 12/29/64*

"We need a real death penalty, one that will actually work. If you read the papers or listen to the 'forgive and forget' crowd here, you would think that the killers and thugs here are never to blame for their actions."

— *New & Observer, 5/27/90*

"The right to own, manage and secure property is not merely the most sacred of 'human rights'—it is the very basis of civilization. When a country begins to disregard property rights, that is an unfailing symptom of barbarism ahead."

— *Viewpoint, 9/2/68*

"You have a classic delineation between the difference between a liberal and a conservative. (Liberal politicians) don't care about the next generation—they care about the next election. I care a heck of a lot more about the next generation than I do about the next election."
— News & Observer, 10/28/90

"From this night on, I intend to continue my personal pledge that, if elected, I will resist with all the strength and energy I can muster, the destructive tactics of the Teddy Kennedys, the Hubert Humphreys, the Muskies and McGoverns—and all the rest of the wrecking crew now dominating the Senate of the United States."
— On winning the GOP nomination for the U.S. Senate, 5/6/72

"I don't want to be like the hypochondriac who directed the inscription to go on his tombstone that said: 'See, I told you I was sick.' We're not sick, but the nation is going through a political aberration now."

— News & Observer, 10/21/90

"We have had 27 years of social engineering masquerading in the guise of advancing civil rights. The race-conscious politics of the last quarter of a century have done a great deal to benefit a few of the most advantaged minority groups while many more have been left further and further behind."

— News & Observer, 6/27/91

"They will cross our borders with impunity. They don't speak English, they don't have homes, they don't have jobs, they don't have anything but a yearning for freedom, and they go on welfare rolls. If you think we have economic problems now with the bloated welfare programs, just add 100 million people."

— *Speech in Clinton, N.C. 4/14/94*
News & Observer, 4/15/94

"Freedom isn't free. Its prime ingredients are inspiration, dedication and perspiration. The guy who works for a living has neither the time nor the inclination to march in protest movements. But he generally has the energy to reach for the next rung on the ladder of life."

— *Viewpoint, 6/27/66*

"It is a feather in North Carolina's cap for us to be No. 50 (in return of federal tax dollars). We use less of the taxpayers' money for welfare and that sort of thing."

— *Charlotte Observer, 4/21/91*

"This is the season of promising politicians. They come out like cockroaches this season of the year... Let's take a vote: Everybody against clean air, please raise your hand... I love clean air and I love education. But I love fiscal responsibility, or the hope of it, more... If we don't restore this country to fiscal sanity, we can kiss everything good-bye."

— *The Hotline, 9/7/90*

"Liberty in any form is not guaranteed by edicts or proclamations or slogans from the mob, but by order and discipline and fundamental self-control."
— *When Free Men Shall Stand, p.21, 1976*

"Forty-four years an unending barrage of 'deals'—the New Deal, the Fair Deal, the New Frontier, and the Great Society...—have regimented our people and our economy and federalized almost every human enterprise."
— *When Free Men Shall Stand, p. 11, 1976*

"No product and no man's labor ought to be artificially propped up or protected in price."
— *When Free men Shall Stand, p. 40, 1976*

"You cannot solve problems by throwing federal dollars. Washington cannot solve problems anyhow, because Washington is the problem."

— *News & Observer, 9/5/90*

" Nothing comes easier than spending the public money. It appears to belong to nobody, and the temptation is overwhelming to confer it on somebody."

— *When Free Men Shall Stand, p.47, 1976*

MULTICULTURALISM

"Even the blacks, the minorities, acknowledge now that it [desegregation] was highly destructive to their interests. They remember a very fine black school there and had pride in its academics, in its extracurricular things, in its football teams, its basketball teams. That school does not exist for them anymore."
— *News & Observer, 9/23/90*

"The last thing the Senate should do is engage in clearly an inflammatory action. As far as I know, race relations in North Carolina are excellent. They may not be in Illinois or Ohio. I do not know about that, but in North Carolina they are fine."
— *News & Observer, 7/24/93*

"We noticed a news item on the wire the other day. What puzzles us is the question of why, if there is a need for motel rooms for Negroes ... why haven't there been more investments in such enterprises. But the very existence of this need seems to us to point to a clear opportunity of service and, if you'll forgive us for saying so, of profit. But we are yet to hear of any suggestions by any racial organization—NAACP, CORE or any other—that investments in such enterprises be encouraged."

— *Viewpoint, 7/7/62*

"The nation has been hypnotized by the swaying and gesturing of the watusi and the frug."

— *Viewpoint, 3/22/66*

"On the floor we fight hard; we're...free, white and 21, as we say in North Carolina."
— *New York Times, 6/28/81*

"Unless our Negro citizens submit more easily than we predict they will, North Carolina does not have the simple choice between segregated schools and integrated schools. Our only choice is between integrated public schools and free-choice private schools. ...The decision will have been made by a very small minority of people who are hell-bent on forced integration."
— *1955 essay about public school desegregation, News & Observer, 10/31/90*

"You think I'm trying to inject race? Harvey Gantt is black. I'm white. Neither of us chose to be either. If he thinks we've got to keep our mouths shut because he's black ... then he's got a problem. I've got to campaign on who he is and what he is. And I know both now."
— *News & Observer, 11/1/90*

"It's all very well and good to talk about 'uplifting society' but somewhere along the line we must face the fact of life that from the beginning of time a lot of human beings have been born bums."
— *Viewpoint, 12/5/66*

"I think busing is the worst tyranny ever perpetrated on America."
— *News & Observer, 6/17/81*

"An unlawfully pitched tent by Negroes in Mississippi is no less an affront to society than, say, efforts by the Ku Klux Klan to set up camp on the lawns of Broughton High School in Raleigh."

— *Viewpoint, 6/27/66*

"Buildings and houses don't make slums. People do. People who are too lazy to wash and sweep and mop and scrub. People who toss their garbage in the yard, and throw discarded furniture out the window to rot beside empty wine bottles. That's a real assembly line for a slum."

— *Viewpoint, 8/25/66*

"Black power movements are festering on Negro campuses, and among Negro and white beatnik students on integrated campuses. Whether they realize it , they are puppets on a string, being manipulated from far away."

— *Viewpoint, 2/20/68*

"If we don't crack down on this (fraud by some recipients), we're doing a disservice to the poor. This food stamp racket is so big, the Mafia is in it."

— *Los Angeles Times, 12/15/85*

"Some heads would be cracked if anything is done that even appears to be racist. Now, what ya'll call racist is one thing."

— *The Hotline, 8/27/90*

"Martin Luther King repeatedly refers to his 'non-violent movement.' It is about as non-violent as the Marines landing on Iwo Jima."

— *Viewpoint, 3/11/65*

44

NEWS MEDIA

"Observe ... the television reports on almost any protest march or demonstration. Look carefully into the faces of the people participating. What you will see, for the most part, are dirty, unshaven, often crude young men, and stringy-haired awkward young women who cannot attract attention any other way. They are strictly second-rate all the way."

— *Viewpoint, 4/26/68*

"The trouble with our country today is our major media, our politicians and the people supposed to be our leading thinkers have allowed themselves to become saturated with intellectual dishonesty. They are interested only in the rights of atheists and agnostics."

— *Washington Post, 1/24/83*

*"The confederation of liberals had struck out
again: the homosexuals, the defenders of
pornographic artistry — if you want to call it
that — the National Organization for Women,
the pro-abortion crowd, the labor union
bosses, and the left-wing news media."*

— *News & Observer, 6/1/91*

*"I'm sorry I'm late, but I've been home
watching the grieving face of Dan Rather.
There's no joy in Mudville tonight. The
mighty ultraliberal establishment—the liberal
politicians and editors and commentators and
columnists—have struck out again."*

— *News & Observer, 11/7/90*

"I've got several holes in my head: one, two three. It shows you what the artists can do. They can't even get the holes in the right place."

— Charlotte Observer, 8/31/90

"People who believe in the Lord and who don't like homosexuality, and who don't like taxpayers being required to finance filth — they all melded together."

— News & Observer, 11/22/90

"I say this to CBS or anybody else who wants to get tough: If they think they can intimidate us, they better think again. I say again, let 'em try. Let 'em make my day."

— speech, Raleigh, Raleigh Times, 3/25/85

"I'm just not interested in a dog and pony show where you guys [reporters] sit there with loaded questions and think, 'How can I shoot him out of the saddle?'"

— on refusing to participate in candidates forums;
News & Observer, 8/10/90

"I have never seen a socialistic government which the New York Times or the Washington Post did not like. I am ashamed of the major media in my country."

— Washington Post, 7/12/86

DOWN HOME

"You know, I don't want to offend my tobacco friends, but I will parenthetically say that I don't know a single tobacco farmer who smokes now. Maybe he knows what's in the cigarette. But I stopped and had no problem about it."

— News & Observer, 7/31/92

"It is not my political organization. It never has been. I don't run it (the National Congressional Club). ... We get along fine. But I have almost no contact with them. I don't know what they're doing."

— News & Observer, 2/6/94

"I'm not about to sell you (tobacco farmers) down the river now."

— *News & Observer, 1/27/94*

"I like her (Democratic ambassadorial nominee Jeanette Hyde) style even though we come from opposite sides of the political fence."

— *States News Service, 2/26/94*

"It never occurred to me in the most vivid fantasy of my life that I'd ever see happen in North Carolina what happened yesterday (with the GOP taking control of the state House of Representatives)."

— *News & Observer, 11/13/94*

ART

53

"If that's 'chilling censorship' there are a lot of folks around who intend to make the most of it. There is widespread resentment to the American taxpayers' money being wasted on crude, blasphemous and childish 'works of art' by people to whom nothing is sacred."

— Los Angeles Times, 6/23/89

"No artist has a pre-emptive claim on the tax dollars of the American people to put forward such trash. I don't even acknowledge the fellow who did it was an artist. I think he was a jerk."

— New York Times, 7/27/89

"If someone wants to write ugly, nasty things on the men's room wall, the taxpayers do not have to provide the crayons,"

— on public funding of the arts;
New York Times, 7/28/89

JESSE

"I am inclined not to respond to personal attacks, but my father once told me that the best way to determine whether a stick is crooked or not is to lay a straight one beside it."

— Washington Post, 3/18/86

"We were 20 points down ... back in 1984 and it came out all right. I'm not living on a diet of fingernail bites, I'll tell you that."

— News & Observer, 10/21/90

"This senator is not a goody-goody two shoes. I've lived a long time, but every Christian ethic cries out for me to do something. I call a spade a spade, a perverted human being a perverted human being."

— on homosexuality; Los Angeles Times, 10/14/87

"I'm so old-fashioned I believe in horsewhipping."

— News & Observer, 7/19/91

"Let this message go out. I will not yield to threats. I will not be deterred by political misrepresentation or distortion. Others may try to dodge the issue and squirm and flip-flop but not this senator. Let those people explain why they favor destroying these little babies just because they happen to be the wrong sex in the womb."

— The Hotline, 1/15/90

"I've been defeated before ... but this is the first time an amendment I have offered has been defeated by a bunch of bull ... back-room deals and parliamentary flimflam."

— News & Observer, 11/1/91

"(My constituents) sent me to Washington to vote no against excessive federal spending, against forced busing of little schoolchildren, and to vote no against the forces who have driven God out of the classrooms."

— *News & Observer, 6/26/83*

"I am constantly referred to by the artistes and others as a redneck. ... If you want to call me a redneck, that's fine. They're the salt of the earth. I'm proud to be called that."

— *News & Observer, 10/18/90*

"I didn't go to Washington to be a yes man to anybody, any president, Democrat, Republican or independent. And I didn't go there to be Mr. Popularity. I didn't go there to participate in the cocktail parties and the social circuit. I went there with a set of principles that I believe deserve to survive."
— *News & Observer, 10/21/90*

"I have been so intrigued that I have been called repeatedly the Prince of Darkness because of my efforts to restore school prayer, and I'm called a right-wing extremist because I try to stand up for the most innocent and helpless of humans—the unborn children."
— *speech, Greensboro, News & Observer, 11/3/84*

"The far-out liberals have hit North Carolina like swarms of political locusts. In just one week's time, the liberals have spent $200,000 for a massive TV blitz designed to defeat their number one target—Jesse Helms."
— News & Observer, 9/4/90

"They don't support me, fair enough. A lot of people don't support me. I just hope more than 50 percent of the people do support me."
— News & Observer, 8/29/90

"I've always been a man who played principle over politics and if I lose, let them say about me: 'Jesse—he never gave an inch.'"
— Life, 12/83

"There are far worse things than being defeated for re-election in the U.S. Senate. Selling your soul to get elected is one of them. I will not turn my back on the millions of unborn children to placate the liberal feminists, the Molly Yard people. I will not retreat."

— News & Observer, 10/14/90

"The Lord did not make me impossible of error. All I've had to offer you is the total dedication in serving you as best I know how. And I've always leveled with you, and always will, knowing full well that everyone will not agree with me."

— campaign debate, News & Observer, 7/30/84

"I can be flippant and say that it is a lot easier to throw grenades than it is to catch them. You spend a lot of time in a chairmanship that even other senators don't realize. It is like running a business."

— News & Observer, 11/16/86

"You'll be called Senator No (for voting against federal spending bills), but it can be done and it must be done if our young people have any chance of continuing to live in freedom and in abundance."

— News & Observer, 4/20/84

"If [the Lord] took me five minutes from now, He's still given me more than I deserve."

— News & Observer, 7/27/92

"On the issues I am precisely where I was 20 years ago, 30 years ago. I don't think anybody has ever accused me of changing my principles."

— *News & Observer, 2/8/81*

"Of course I'm impressed and deeply touched. I hope it (the Jesse Helms Center in Wingate, N.C.) serves a useful purpose to encourage people to think about the meaning of the miracle of America."

— *Associated Press, 4/23/94*

"I have done my best as a senator to (filibuster) hold up legislation I thought was not in the best interest of the country. Don't you believe these guys who say, 'We want to do the nation's business.' What they are saying is, 'Let's pass the things we want passed. Let's spend the money we want spent. ... (The number of filibusters) hasn't increased enough to suit me. I want to challenge more things. I want to challenge more spending."
— Charlotte Observer, 6/18/94

THE QUOTE FLAP

"OH, *THAT* ONE? THAT'S JUST JESSE POPPING OFF AT THE MEDIA..."

"Well, well, I — you know, you asked an honest question (Is President Clinton up to the job of commander-in-chief?). I'll give you an honest answer. No, I do not, and neither do the people in the armed forces."

— CNN, 11/19/94

"I don't know that the First Amendment excludes anyone. I was asked a question on nationwide television that I did not expect. I either had to dodge it or lie or tell the truth, and I always opt to tell the truth. ... Mr. Clinton better watch out if he comes down here. He'd better have a bodyguard."

— News & Observer, 11/22/94

"I made a mistake last evening which I shall not repeat. In an informal telephone interview with a local reporter I made an offhand remark in an attempt to emphasize how strongly the American people feel about the nation's declining defense capability and other issues in which the president has been involved and for which he is responsible."

— *News & Observer, 11/23/94*

"I don't have a tape recorder. I'm not going to be interviewed without my own tape recorder."

— *News & Observer, 12/2/94*

"It was a non-story and you knew it. It was never a threat and everybody knew that. If you're asking me if it was a threat, you know it was not a threat. ... These liberal elitists shot themselves in the foot. The American people don't trust the news media. You ought to know. You see what they do to tobacco every day."

— *Associated Press, 12/7/94*

OTHER ISSUES

"To be blunt about it, the Department of Agriculture is being overrun by homosexuals, and they have been running the store to a great extent."

— *Charlotte Observer, 10/16/94*

"With a $4.6 trillion federal debt, Congress is now being asked ... to give an unlimited — I repeat, an unlimited — authorization for an unlimited number of years for a new (African-American) museum."

— *Knight-Ridder News Service, 10/9/94*

"The people who supported me through the years have been, in my opinion, taken advantage of. Helms for Senate was a cow to be milked. ...People would call me up, and say, 'Jesse, what's going on?' ... I just got sick of it. It was implicit in so many (fund raising) letters: 'Oh, we have got to have so much money. Otherwise Jesse's going down in flames.' And Jesse never saw any money. I didn't need any money."

— *Charlotte Observer, 10/2/94*

"(Students) can't pray in school, but you can hand out condoms to them. What kind of message does this send to them?"

— *Associated Press, 2/5/94*

"I am not going to stand idly by when a good and decent man is persecuted by homosexuals in the USDA."

— *News & Observer, 10/19/94*

"Law and order is what everybody talks about, but what few people do anything about."

— *News & Observer, 3/27/94*

ILLUSTRATED
JESSE

by

HELMS TAKES OVER MEDIA — WHAT IF? DEPARTMENT.

UNGH AND OOOGAH WONDER IF JESSE HAS BECOME TOO CONSERVATIVE FOR THEM...

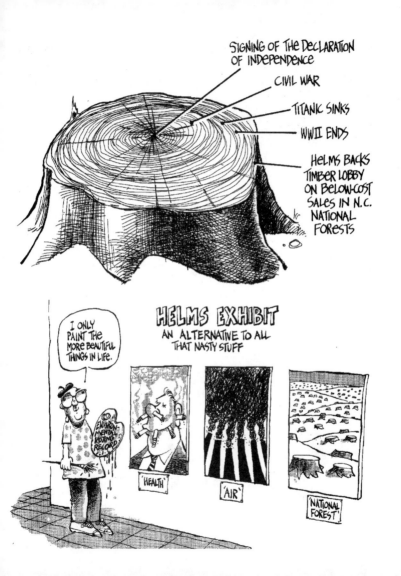

HELMS POLITICAL DICTIONARY

THE GOOD,
THE BAD,
AND THE UGLY
AMERICAN.
STARRING
JESSE HELMS

COMING ATTRACTIONS:
'A MOUTHFUL OF RHETORIC'
'FOR A FEW HOLLERS MORE'

PRODUCED BY NORTH CAROLINA ELECTIONS

MEXICO

SENATOR ON BOARD

'JESSE, DON'T YOU THINK YOU'RE TAKING YOURSELF A BIT SERIOUSLY THESE DAYS?'